50 Best-Loved

CHRISTMAS

FAVORITES

Easy to Sing, Easy to Play

Arranged by David McDonald

Lillenas PUBLISHING COMPANY
KANSAS CITY, MO 64141

www.lillenas.com

1

O Come, All Ye Faithful

Traditional Latin Hymn

JOHN F. WADE
Arr. by David McDonald

Go, Tell It on the Mountain

JOHN W. WORK, JR.

Spiritual
Arr. by David McDonald

Sing We Now of Christmas

Traditional French Carol
Arr. by David McDonald

With movement

Silent Night! Holy Night!

4

JOSEPH MOHR

FRANZ GRUBER
Arr. by David McDonald

We Three Kings

Words and Music by
JOHN H. HOPKINS, JR.
Arr. by David McDonald

still pro-ceed-ing, Guide us to thy per-fect light.

The Friendly Beasts

6

Traditional English Carol
Arr. by David McDonald

Gently

Je-sus our bro-ther, kind and good Was hum-bly

born in a sta-ble rude, And the friend-ly beasts a-

round Him stood, Je-sus our bro-ther, kind and good.

7 O Little Town of Bethlehem

PHILLIPS BROOKS

LEWIS H. REDNER
Arr. by David McDonald

Good Christian Men, Rejoice

8

Traditional Latin Carol

Traditional German Carol
Arr. by David McDonald

9   Come, Thou Long-Expected Jesus

CHARLES WESLEY

ROWLAND H. PRICHARD
Arr. by David McDonald

10 Away in a Manger

Anonymous

JAMES R. MURRAY
Arr. by David McDonald

Gently

A - way in a man - ger, no crib for a bed, The

lit - tle Lord Je - sus laid down His sweet head. The

stars in the sky looked down where He lay, The

lit - tle Lord Je - sus a - sleep on the hay.

Angels We Have Heard on High

Traditional French Carol
Arr. by David McDonald

Angels we have heard on high, Sweet-ly sing-ing o'er the plains,

And the moun-tains in re-ply, Ech-o-ing their joy-ous strains.

Glo - - - - ri - a

in ex-cel-sis De - o! Glo - - -

- - ri - a in ex-cel-sis De - o!

12

O Come, O Come Emmanuel

Traditional Latin Hymn

Plainsong
Arr. by David McDonald

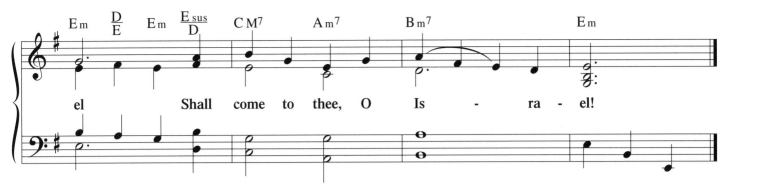

el   Shall come to thee, O Is - ra - el!

I Saw Three Ships

13

Traditional English Carol
Arr. by David McDonald

I saw three ships come sail - ing in, On

Christ - mas day, on Christ - mas day; I saw three ships come

sail - ing in, On Christ - mas day in the morn - ing.

14

He Is Born

Traditional French Carol
Arr. by David McDonald

He is born, the— ho-ly Child; Play the— o-boe and bag-pipes mer-ri-ly!

He is born, the— ho-ly Child; Sing we— all of the Sav-ior mild.

Thro' long a-ges— of the past, Proph-ets have fore-told His com-ing;

Thro' long a-ges— of the past, Now the time has— come at last!

It Came upon the Midnight Clear

EDMUND H. SEARS

RICHARD S. WILLIS
Arr. by David McDonald

16   The Birthday of a King

Words and Music by
WILLIAM HAROLD NEIDLINGER
Arr. by David McDonald

sky was bright with a ho - ly light; 'Twas the birth - day of a King.

O Come, Let Us Adore Him 17

Traditional Latin Hymn

JOHN F. WADE
Arr. by David McDonald

Worshipful

O come, let us a - dore Him! O come, let us a - dore Him! O come, let us a - dore Him, Christ, the Lord!

18   O Holy Night

JOHN S. DWIGHT

ADOLPHE C. ADAM
Arr. by David McDonald

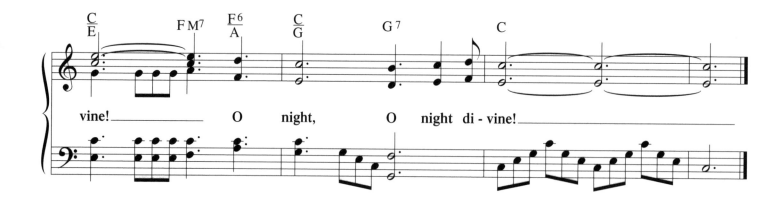

vine!_____ O night, O night di - vine!_____

19 That Beautiful Name

JEAN PERRY

MABEL JOHNSTON CAMP
Arr. by David McDonald

I know of a name, A beau - ti - ful

name, That an - gels bro't down to earth;_____

_____ They whis - pered it low, One night long a -

Child in the Manger

MARY MACDONALD

Traditional Gaelic Melody
Arr. by David McDonald

How Great Our Joy!

Traditional German Carol
Arr. by David McDonald

22   We Wish You a Merry Christmas

Traditional English Carol
Arr. by David McDonald

Good King Wenceslas

JOHN M. NEALE

Traditional
Arr. by David McDonald

Good King Wen - ces - las looked out On the feast of Ste - phen,

When the snow lay 'round a - bout, Deep and crisp and e - ven.

Bright - ly shone the moon that night, Tho' the frost was cru - el.

When a poor man came in sight, Gath - 'ring win - ter fu - el.

24 What Child Is This?

William C. Dix

Traditional English Melody
Arr. by David McDonald

Haste, haste to bring Him laud, The Babe, the Son of Mar - y.

The Coventry Carol

25

Traditional English Carol
Arr. by David McDonald

Gently

Lul - lay, Thou lit - tle, ti - ny Child. By, by, lul -

ly, lul - lay. Lul - lay, Thou lit - tle,

ti - ny Child. By, by, lul - ly, lul - lay.

Carol of the Bells

Traditional Ukranian Carol
Arr. by David McDonald

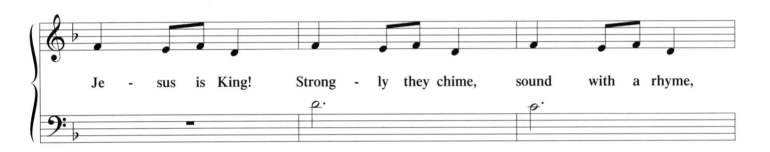

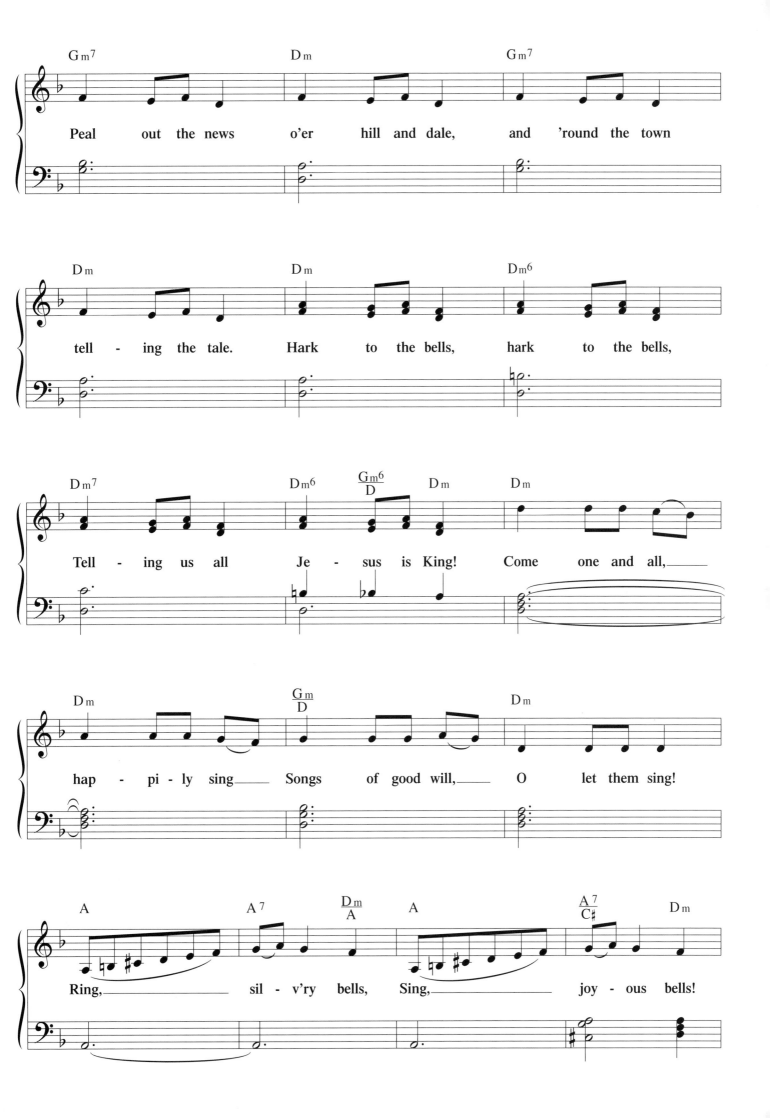

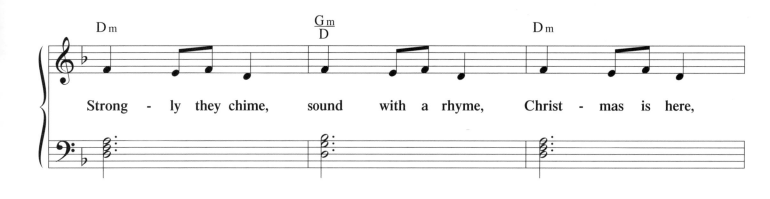

Strong - ly they chime, sound with a rhyme, Christ - mas is here,

wel - come the King! Hark to the bells, hark to the bells,

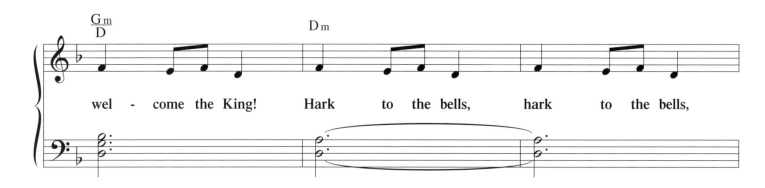

Tell - ing us all Je - sus is King! Ring! Ring! bells.

27 The First Noel

Traditional English Carol

W. Sandy's *Christmas Carols*
Arr. by David McDonald

The first No - el the an - gels did

28 Thou Didst Leave Thy Throne

EMILY E. S. ELLIOTT

TIMOTHY R. MATTHEWS
Arr. by David McDonald

Worshipful

WILLIAM C. DIX

CONRAD KOCHER
Arr. by David McDonald

As with gladness men of old Did the guiding
light behold, As with joy they hailed its light–
Leading onward, beaming bright, So, most gracious
Lord, may we Evermore be led to Thee.

30 There's a Song in the Air

JOSIAH G. HOLLAND

KARL P. HARRINGTON
Arr. by David McDonald

Bring a Torch, Jeanette, Isabella

Traditional
Arr. by David McDonald

32 Once in Royal David's City

CECIL F. ALEXANDER

HENRY J. GAUNTLETT
Arr. by David McDonald

Celebrate Immanuel's Name

33

CHARLES WESLEY

Foundery Collection
Arr. by David McDonald

34 O Sing a Song of Bethlehem

LOUIS F. BENSON

English Melody
Arr. by David McDonald

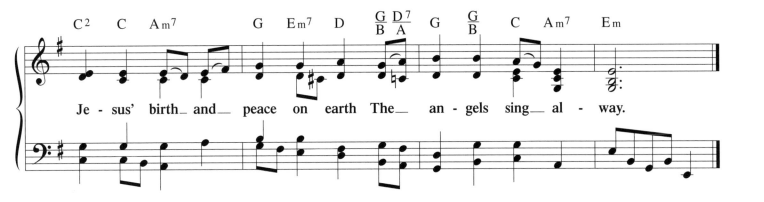

I Heard the Bells on Christmas Day 35

HENRY WADSWORTH LONGFELLOW

JEAN BAPTISTE CALKIN
Arr. by David McDonald

36   Angels, from the Realms of Glory

JAMES MONTGOMERY

HENRY T. SMART
Arr. by David McDonald

Still, Still, Still

37

Traditional Austrian Carol
Arr. by David McDonald

38 Let All Mortal Flesh Keep Silence

Liturgy of St. James

Traditional French Carol
Arr. by David McDonald

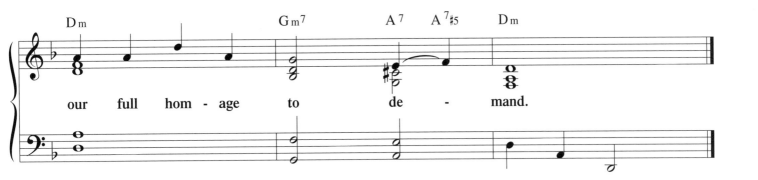

our full hom - age to de - mand.

While Shepherds Watched Their Flocks 39

NAHUM TATE

GEORGE FREDERICK HANDEL
Arr. by David McDonald

While__ shep - herds watched their flocks by__ night, All__ seat - ed on the__

ground,_____ The__ an - gel of the Lord came__ down, And__

glo - ry shone a - round,_____ And glo - ry shone a - round.

40   Joy to the World

ISAAC WATTS

GEORGE FREDERICK HANDEL
Arr. by David McDonald

Joyfully

Joy to the world! the Lord is come; Let earth re - ceive her King._____ Let ev - 'ry___ heart___ pre - pare___ Him room,_____ And heav'n and na - ture___ sing, And___ heav'n and na - ture___ sing, And___ heav'n,_____ and heav'n_____ and na - ture sing.

O Sanctissima

Traditional Sicilian Carol
Arr. by David McDonald

PLEASE NOTE: Copying of this product is not covered by CCLI licenses. For CCLI information call 1-800-234-2446.

42 Away in a Manger

Anonymous

WILLIAM J. KIRKPATRICK
Arr. by David McDonald

Gentle Mary Laid Her Child

43

JOSEPH SIMPSON COOK

Traditional
Arr. by David McDonald

44   Hark! the Herald Angels Sing

CHARLES WESLEY

FELIX MENDELSSOHN
Arr. by David McDonald

Fum, Fum, Fum

45

Traditional Spanish Carol
Arr. by David McDonald

O Come, Little Children

46

Words and Music by
JOHANN A. P. SCHULZ
Arr. by David McDonald

Gently

O come, lit-tle chil-dren, O come, one and all, To Beth-le-hem's sta-ble, in Beth-le-hem's stall, And see with re-joic-ing this glo-ri-ous sight, Our Fa-ther in heav-en has sent us this night.

Infant Holy, Infant Lowly

Traditional Polish Carol
Arr. by David McDonald

48   Here We Come A-Caroling

Traditional English Carol
Arr. by David McDonald

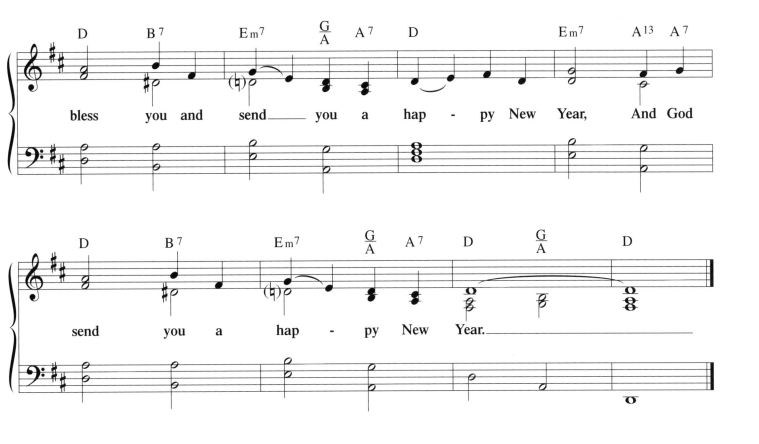

bless you and send you a hap - py New Year, And God

send you a hap - py New Year.

Rise Up, Shepherd, and Follow

49

African-American Spiritual
Arr. by David McDonald

There's a star in the East on Christ - mas morn.

Rise up, shep - herd and fol - low. It will

God Rest You Merry, Gentlemen

Traditional English Carol
Arr. by David McDonald

ALPHABETICAL INDEX

Angels We Have Heard on High . . . 11

Angels, from the Realms of Glory . . 36

As with Gladness Men of Old 29

Away in a Manger
(Tune: AWAY IN A MANGER) . . 10

Away in a Manger
(Tune: CRADLE SONG) 42

Bring a Torch, Jeanette, Isabella 31

Carol of the Bells 26

Celebrate Immanuel's Name 33

Child in the Manger 20

Come, Thou Long-Expected Jesus . . 9

Fum, Fum, Fum 45

Gentle Mary Laid Her Child 43

Go, Tell It on the Mountain 2

God Rest You Merry, Gentlemen . . . 50

Good Christian Men, Rejoice 8

Good King Wenceslas 23

Hark! the Herald Angels Sing 44

He Is Born 14

Here We Come A-Caroling 48

How Great Our Joy 21

I Heard the Bells on Christmas Day . 35

I Saw Three Ships 13

Infant Holy, Infant Lowly 47

It Came upon the Midnight Clear . . 15

Joy to the World 40

Let All Mortal Flesh Keep Silence . . 38

O Come, All Ye Faithful 1

O Come, Let Us Adore Him 17

O Come, Little Children 46

O Come, O Come Emmanuel 12

O Holy Night 18

O Little Town of Bethlehem 7

O Sanctissima 41

O Sing a Song of Bethlehem 34

Once in Royal David's City 32

Rise Up, Shepherd, and Follow 49

Silent Night! Holy Night! 4

Sing We Now of Christmas 3

Still, Still, Still 37

That Beautiful Name 19

The Birthday of a King 16

The Coventry Carol 25

The First Noel 27

The Friendly Beasts 6

There's a Song in the Air 30

Thou Didst Leave Thy Throne 28

We Three Kings 5

We Wish You a Merry Christmas . . . 22

What Child Is This? 24

While Shepherds Watched
Their Flocks 39